In the Fall

Written by Larry Dane Brimner • Illustrated by R. W. Alley

Published in the United States of America by The Child's World®
PO Box 326 • Chanhassen, MN 55317-0326
800-599-READ • www.childsworld.com

Reading Adviser

Cecilia Minden-Cupp, PhD, Director of Language and Literacy, Harvard University Graduate School
of Education, Cambridge, Massachusetts

Acknowledgments

The Child's World®: Mary Berendes, Publishing Director

Editorial Directions, Inc.: E. Russell Primm, Editorial Director and Project Manager; Katie Marsico,
Associate Editor; Judith Shiffer, Assistant Editor; Matt Messbarger, Editorial Assistant

The Design Lab: Kathleen Petelinsek, Design and Art Production

Library of Congress Cataloging-in-Publication Data

Brimner, Larry Dane.
  In the fall / written by Larry Dane Brimner ; illustrated by R.W. Alley.
     p. cm. — (Magic door to learning)
  Summary: A young child describes the sights and sounds of autumn, including the "Chop! Chop!" of
the woodcutter and the changing colors of the leaves.
  ISBN 1-59296-517-2 (library bound : alk. paper) [1. Autumn—Fiction.] I. Alley, R. W. (Robert W.),
ill. II. Title.
  PZ7.B767Inat 2005
  [E]—dc22   2005005361

A book is a door, a magic door.
It can take you places
you have never been before.
Ready? Set?
Turn the page.
Open the door.
Now it is time to explore.

Fall is the time of year
when leaves change colors
and swirl in the wind.

Chop! Chop! Chop!

We hear the far-off
sound of the woodcutter.

7

A fire will warm him during
the long winter ahead.

Down by the river, we see the first hint of ice on the pond. It's time to get our skates ready for cold, snowy winter!

I dig my ice skates
out of my closet.
They do not fit this
year—not even when
I curl up my toes!
Mom says we will
buy new ones.

13

Mom stuffs paper into my
too-small skates, and my little
brother tries them on.

They are just his size!

When he tries
to stand up,
he wobbles
and topples

and we all have a fit of giggles.

In the fall,
when days
get shorter
and nights
grow longer

and leaves swirl in the wind
as we get ready
for winter.

23

Our story is over, but there is still much to explore beyond the magic door!

How many different kinds of leaves can you find in the fall? When it's autumn and the leaves begin to drop, build your own leaf collection. Be sure to pick leaves that are different colors, shapes, and sizes.

These books will help you explore at the library and at home:

dePaola, Tomie. *Four Friends in Autumn.* New York: Simon & Schuster Books for Young Readers, 2004.

Hall, Zoe, and Shari Halpern (illustrator). *Fall Leaves Fall!* New York: Scholastic Press, 2000.

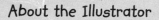

About the Author

Larry Dane Brimner is an award-winning author of more than 120 books for children. When he isn't at his computer writing, he can be found biking in Colorado or hiking in Arizona. You can visit him online at *www.brimner.com.*

About the Illustrator

R. W. Alley has illustrated more than seventy-five books for children and has authored five of these. Since 1997, he has served as the illustrator on Michael Bond's Paddington Bear series. Alley lives in Barrington, Rhode Island, with his wife and two children. He often visits local elementary schools to discuss how words and pictures come together to form books.